BRAVE GIRL

Clara and the
Shirtwaist Makers' Strike of 1909

Written by Michelle Markel   Illustrated by Melissa Sweet

BALZER + BRAY

An Imprint of HarperCollins*Publishers*

Balzer + Bray is an imprint of HarperCollins Publishers.

Brave Girl: Clara and the Shirtwaist Makers' Strike of 1909
Text copyright © 2013 by Michelle Markel
Illustrations copyright © 2013 by Melissa Sweet
Library of Congress Cataloging-in-Publication Data is available.
ISBN 978-0-06-180442-7

The artist used watercolor, gouache, and mixed media to create the illustrations for this book.
Typography by Rachel Zegar
12 13 14 15 16 SCP 10 9 8 7 6 5 4 3 2 1
❖
First Edition

For workers everywhere

—M.M.

For Cathy

—M.S.

A steamship pulls into the harbor,
carrying hundreds of immigrants—and a
surprise for New York City.

The surprise is dirt poor, just five feet tall, and
hardly speaks a word of English.
Her name is Clara Lemlich.
This girl's got grit, and she's going to prove it.
Look out, New York!

Clara knows in her bones what is right and what is wrong.

What's wrong begins a few weeks after the Lemlichs move into their tenement in America.

No one will hire Clara's father.

They will, however, hire Clara.

That's right—Clara. Companies are hiring thousands of immigrant girls to make blouses, coats, nightgowns, and other women's clothing. They earn only a few dollars a month, but it helps pay for food and rent. So instead of carrying books to school, many girls carry sewing machines to work. Clara becomes a garment worker.

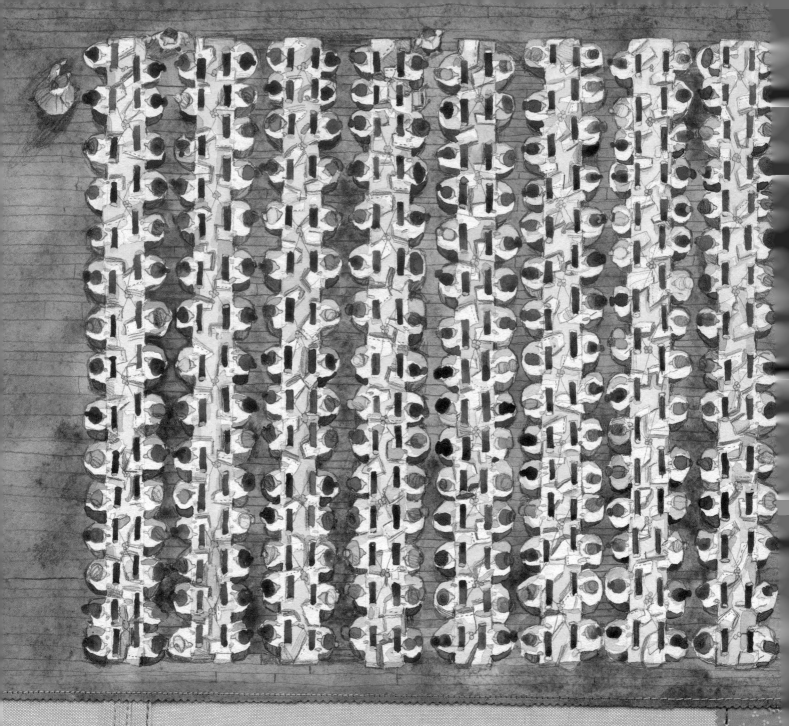

From dawn to dusk, she's locked up in a factory. Rows and rows of young women bend over their tables, stitching collars, sleeves, and cuffs as fast as they can. "Hurry up, hurry up," the bosses yell. *Ratatatatat*, hisses Clara's machine. The sunless room is stuffy from all the bodies crammed inside. There are two filthy toilets, one sink, and three towels for three hundred girls to share.

Saturday, _August_ 1909

Clara learns the rules.
If you're a few minutes late,
you lose half a day's pay.

If you prick your finger and bleed
on the cloth, you're fined. If it happens
a second time, you're fired.

The doors are locked, and you're
inspected every night before you
leave to be sure you haven't stolen
anything from the factory.

But Clara
is uncrushable.

She wants to read, she wants to learn! At the end of her
shift, though her eyes hurt from straining in the gaslight and
her back hurts from hunching over the sewing machine, she
walks to the library.

She fills her empty stomach with a single glass of
milk and goes to school at night. When she gets home
in the late evening, she sleeps only a few hours before
rising again.

As the weeks grind by, Clara makes friends with the other factory girls. At lunch, they share stories and secrets as if they were in school, where they belong. Clara smolders with anger, not just for herself, but for all the factory girls, working like slaves. This was not the America she'd imagined.

The men at the factory tell her they've been trying to get the workers to team up in a union. Then they'd strike—refuse to work—until the bosses treat them better. But the men don't think the ladies are tough enough.

Not tough enough?
Because they're girls?
Oh, yes, they are. Clara knows it.
She'll show them.

From then on, at the sewing tables and on the street corners, Clara urges the girls to fight for their rights.

When the seamstresses are overworked, she says, "Strike!"
When they're underpaid, she says, "Strike!"
When they're punished for speaking up, she cries, "Strike!"

And the girls do!

Each time Clara leads a walkout, the bosses fire
her. Each time she pickets, her life is in danger.

The bosses hire men to beat
her and the other strikers.

The police arrest her seventeen times.

They break six of her ribs,
but they can't break her spirit.
It's shatterproof.

Clara hides her bruises from her parents.

A few days later, she's on the picket line again.

And the other girls think, *If she can do it, we can do it too.*

For weeks the small strikes go on. But the bosses find other
young women to do the work for the same low pay and long hours.

We must do something bigger, think Clara and other union leaders. *Something huge. A giant strike, at every garment factory in the city.*

The union holds a meeting. Throngs of workers pack the seats, the aisles, the walls—the hall thrums with excitement. Clara listens to speech after speech.

The speakers, mostly men, want everyone to be careful.
Two hours pass. No one recommends a general strike.
Finally, the most powerful union leader in the country
goes up to the podium. Not even he proposes action!
So Clara does.

That's right—Clara. She calls out from the front of the
hall. The crowd lifts her to the stage, where she shouts
in Yiddish:

"I have no further patience for talk—I move that we go on a general strike!"

And she starts the largest walkout of women workers in U.S. history.

The next morning, New York City is stunned by the sight of
thousands of young women streaming from the factories.

One newspaper calls it an army. Others call it a revolt. It's
a revolt of girls, for some are only twelve years old,

and the rest are barely out of their teens.

   In the coming weeks, Clara is called a hero. She lights up chilly union
halls with her fiery pep talks. Her singing lifts the spirits of the picketers.
When a group of thugs approaches, she yells, "Stand fast, girls!"

And they do. All winter long, in the bitter cold, in their cheap, thin coats, tired and starving and scared, the girls walk alongside the men on the icy sidewalks of the picket line. They spill out of the union halls, blocking the roads, filling street corners and public squares.

Newspapers write stories about them.

College girls raise money for them.

Rich women—swathed in fur coats—picket with the factory girls.

By the time the strike is over, hundreds of bosses agree to let their staff form unions. They shorten the workweek and raise salaries.

The strike emboldens thousands of women to walk out of garment factories in Philadelphia and Chicago.

And the strike convinces Clara to
keep fighting for the rights of workers.
Her throat is hoarse, her feet are sore,
but she has helped thousands of people.
Proving that in America,
wrongs can be righted,
warriors can wear skirts and blouses,
and the bravest hearts
may beat in girls
only five feet tall.

MORE ABOUT THE GARMENT INDUSTRY

Between 1880 and 1920, two million Jews immigrated to America, fleeing persecution, pogroms (government-sanctioned attacks), and poverty in Russia, Ukraine, Poland, and other parts of Eastern Europe. Many of these immigrants found work in the booming garment industry. In 1909, the year of the general strike, nearly four hundred factories employing forty thousand people made blouses for half the country. Of these workers, 80 percent were female, 70 percent were between sixteen and twenty-five years of age, and 65 percent were Russian/Eastern European Jewish (the remainder of workers were Italian and American). Many of the factory owners were Eastern European Jews who had worked their way up in the business.

Abuses were rampant throughout the industry. Many bosses shaved time off lunch hours, set clocks back at the end of the day to fool the workers, made them work long hours—including illegal evening work—for little money, forced them to pay for cloth soiled with blood or spilled food, and fired them at will. Some factories hired girls as young as six years old to cut threads from garments.

At the beginning of the 1909 strike, police and judges sided with the affluent factory owners. Six hundred young women were arrested, and thirteen girls, one as young as twelve years old, were sentenced to five days in the workhouse. Police brutality ceased only when members of the Women's Trade Union League, made up of wealthy and middle-class women, joined the picketers and held meetings to publicize their plight.

When the strike ended, 339 waist and dress manufacturing firms allowed workers to form unions, shortened their workweek, and increased their hourly wages. Some companies refused to negotiate, notably the Triangle Waist Factory, where the following year hazardous conditions led to a fire that claimed 146 lives. The tragedy raised public awareness even further about the evils of the garment industry. (Clara Lemlich, then in her early twenties, investigated health and safety conditions in the garment district for the union.)

In the aftermath of the strike, thousands of workers in Philadelphia—as well as in Chicago, Cleveland, and Kalamazoo—struck for better working conditions or campaigned for the right to organize unions. Along with Clara, fellow strikers Pauline Newman and Rose Schneiderman took on leadership roles in the labor movement. The progress made by the garment industry activists affected jobs throughout the country.

Though there are still wrongs to be righted, today's workers have five-day workweeks, overtime pay, and other protections due in great part to labor leaders like Clara Lemlich and the thousands of brave girls who picketed in the winter of 1909.

SELECTED BIBLIOGRAPHY

General Sources:

Baum, Charlotte, Paula Hyman, and Sonya Michel. *The Jewish Woman in America*. New York: New American Library, 1977.

Diner, Hasia, and Beryl Lieff Benderly. *Her Works Praise Her: A History of Jewish Women in America from Colonial Times to the Present*. New York: Basic Books, 2002.

Howe, Irving. *World of Our Fathers*. New York: Harcourt Brace Jovanovich, 1976.

Marcus, Jacob. *The American Jewish Woman: A Documentary History*. New York: Ktav Publishing House; Cincinnati: American Jewish Archives, 1981.

Marrin, Albert. *Flesh and Blood So Cheap: The Triangle Fire and Its Legacy*. New York: Knopf Books for Young Readers, 2011.

Orleck, Annelise. *Common Sense and a Little Fire: Women and Working Class Politics in the United States, 1900-1965*. Chapel Hill: University of North Carolina Press, 1995.

Scheier, Paula. "Clara Lemlich Shavelson: Fifty Years in Labor's Front Line," *Jewish Life,* November 1954.

Schneiderman, Rose. *All for One*. New York: Paul S. Eriksson, 1967.

Stein, Leon. *Out of the Sweatshop: The Struggle for Industrial Democracy*. New York: Quadrangle/New York Times Book Co., 1977.

Tenement Museum, New York City.

Von Drehle, David. *Triangle: The Fire That Changed America*. New York: Atlantic Monthly Press, 2003.

Weinberg, Sydney Stahl. *The World of Our Mothers: The Lives of Jewish Immigrant Women*. Chapel Hill: University of North Carolina Press, 1988.

Primary Sources:

Lemlich, Clara. *New York Call*, March 28, 1911.

———. *New York Evening Journal*, November 28, 1909.

———. "The Inside of a Shirtwaist Factory: An Appeal to Women Who Wear Choice and Beautiful Clothing," *Good Housekeeping,* 54, No. 3 (March 1912).

Lemlich Shavelson, Clara, to Morris Schappes, March 15, 1965, published in *Jewish Currents* 36, No. 10 (November 1982).